AF480171

Careers for Girls

Let go the sandbags and dream BIG

Writer and illustrator, Anne Daly

CKD Press
Stradbally
Ireland

This book is meant as a source of information and reference for the reader. However, it is not meant as a replacement for the direct expert assistance that a professional career guidance councillor might offer. This book's purpose is to educate, inform, inspire and entertain parents, carers and especially children. While it should be helpful, no book can tell you everything you want to know about every career, considering the number of different countries, cultures, responsibilities and standards there are around the world.

The main career illustrations in this book are there merely to show readers the possibility of what a career could look like, somewhere in the world. Names, characters, businesses, places, events and incidents are the product of the author's imagination and used in a fictitious manner. Any resemblance to actual persons, living or dead, or to actual events or places is purely coincidental and unintentional. However, some real place names, such as the Cliffs of Moher, Newgrange and the Skelligs were used as fun references for background illustrations. The 'Rock of Castlemaise' does exist in a different name but is not near the sea, is in ruins, and unfortunately does not have a café or cable car. However, it does have a stunning view on a sunny day.

ISBN 978-1-7398175-0-3 (hbk)

This books details have been registered with BDSLive.co.uk.
For Cataloguing:
Daly, Anne.
Careers For Girls : Let go the sandbags and dream BIG / Anne Daly.
ISBN 978-1-7398175-0-3 (hbk)

Juvenile Nonfiction / Informational / Expository Descriptive

BISAC CODES:

JNF 011000 - Careers

JNF 053180 - Disabilities & Special needs

JNF 050000 - School & Education

JNF 069000 - Diversity & Multiculture

JNF 023000 - Girls & Women

First Edition 2021

10 9 8 7 6 5 4 3 2 1

Cover design/illustration, layout, typography, graphics, illustrations and written content by Anne Daly. All logos, poems and characters in this book, including but not limited to Recycle Michael©, Paediatric Patrick©, the CKD Press Bug©, 'Girls Supporting Girls'©, 'We Stick Together'©, Knick Knack Basket-Rack©, Knick Knack Medi-Pack©, 'Tap Water'©, are by Anne Daly 2021. 'Hawkenhorn'© is by Kayla Daly 2021. Non-fiction, Informational expository descriptive, 10,000 words. Made with Scribus 1.5.5/1.5.6 and thirty free fonts.

Note: The words **parent** and **girl** are used a lot in this book. **Parents** are the people who are a child's main carers. They can be any gender and can have any biological connection or none at all. The word **girl** means anyone who identifies as a girl.

To every single girl in the world, I say …

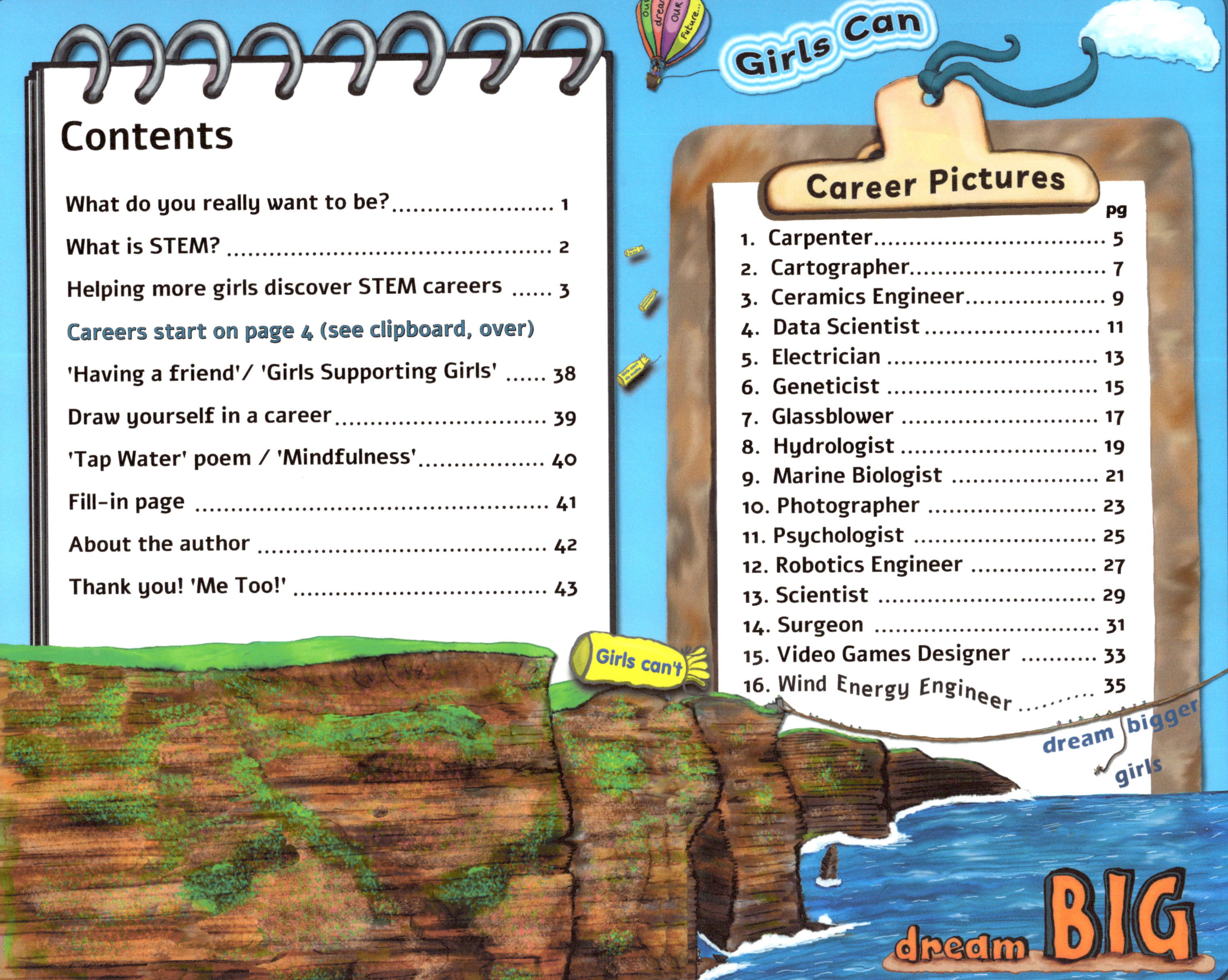

Contents

Career Pictures

Let go the sandbags holding you back.

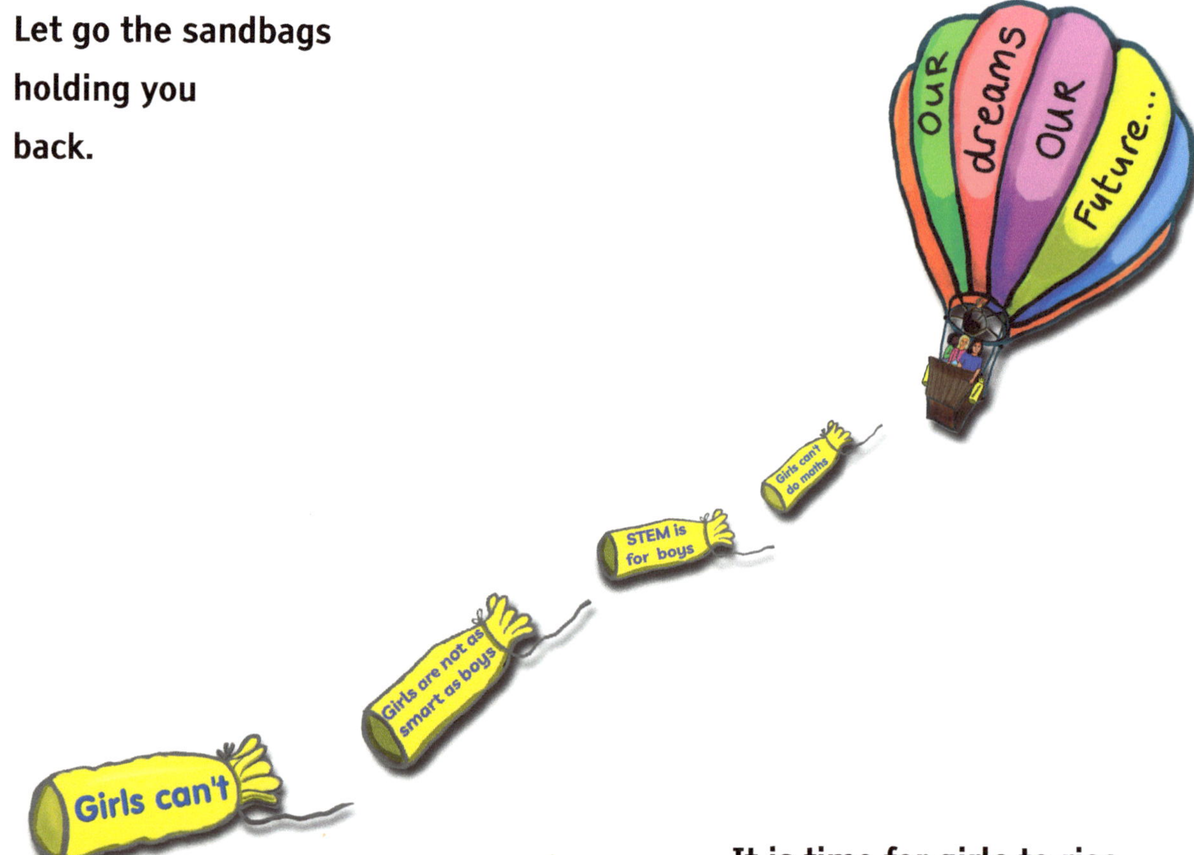

It is time for girls to rise ...

What do you really want to be?

When a teacher asked her class of ten-year-old girls the classic question; **'What do you want to be when you grow up?'** eighteen of those twenty-two girls chose singer, dancer or baker as a career. One girl asked: 'What else can I be? What jobs can women do?'

For many girls, it's hard to imagine themselves having a career, especially in non-traditional areas for women, such as Science, Technology, Engineering or Mathematics (STEM). Thanks in part to modern media, some girls believe that dancing, singing, being famous, marrying someone famous, or becoming a rich sensation, are the only options for success. There are many ways to be successful, and there are many other types of success. Especially in the STEM sector, which offers girls another type of reward.

They may not seem as flashy, but STEM jobs can create opportunities for girls to become important in their field of work, contribute to greater movements, invent new technology, discover new medicines, inspire others and choose a career to help save people, animals or the planet.

And girls can still sing, dance and bake in their spare time, or have more than one career if they want to. Girls have more choices than they know.

If you show girls where they can end up they will dream big enough to get there

A young girl's confidence in herself, and how she thinks society sees her, greatly affects how she imagines her future. If a girl has a positive vision of her future self, then she has a dream that can pull her along and lift her over the many difficulties she might encounter along the way. As her legs and feet get bigger, obstacles will get smaller, and dreams will get closer.

she could rise so high ...

However, too many young women today feel the need to look 'MIO' (media's idea of) pretty, spending much time, effort and money trying to look **'perfect'** all of the time. Girls have a right to help shape the world they are going to live in as adults and they don't need more distractions; they need more support.

They need role models

Since the STEM sector is male-dominated, it will benefit from a greater variety of ideas and opinions that women have to offer. Since boys are already pushed into STEM subjects by parents, teachers and the culture they live in, girls just need a little help getting started. They need someone to show them there is more to their future than how 'perfect' they can look.

Science

Science is everywhere! Healthy food, clean water, medicine, technology, cures for diseases, DNA sequencing, vaccines, communication devices, space exploration, and civilization itself; would not be possible without Science.

Technology

Technology has helped make the dreams of scientists, mathematicians and engineers come true. Telephones, computers, tablets and the internet, have completely transformed our lives and our way of working.

Engineering

Engineering has helped build our cities, bridges, roads, airports and vehicles; and it has also helped develop our technology and communications; and made medical advancements, space travel, renewable energy devices and robotics, possible.

Mathematics

Mathematics is at the heart of all scientific, engineering and technological endeavours. We make sense of the world and the universe through mathematics; and we cannot make any advances, in all areas of life, without this knowledge.

Professor Mark Ferguson, Director General of Science Foundation Ireland, and Chief Scientific Adviser to the government, states: 'As a scientist I am very interested in evidence – data shows that companies that have more equal numbers of men and women in senior positions are more profitable, more innovative, and are better companies than those that are predominantly run by men.' www.irishexaminer.com/lifestyle/arid-20416606.html

There are many studies available online that show why more women are needed in STEM. There is also a shortage of qualified people for STEM job vacancies today. Girls can help to fill those vacancies by choosing STEM subjects in school. If parents and carers know about some of these great careers, they can help young girls discover them. Too many girls choose school subjects without knowing which future doors they may, or may not, open for them.

Of Irish girls surveyed, 65% said their parents are most likely to influence subject choices at school, but only 25% of parents feel 'very informed' about the variety of STEM career opportunities available. More than half stated that they have no experience of modern STEM careers to pass on to their children.

www.iwish.ie/surveys

What are the barriers for girls getting into STEM?

- **Parental influence**
Encouraging only the careers the parents know about.
- **Stereotypes**
Thinking boys are better at maths and engineering.
- **Culture**
Encouraging girls to stick to cultural norms for women.
- **Lack of knowledge**
Not knowing which school subjects lead to which careers.
- **Lack of female role models**
Not seeing enough women in STEM careers.
- **Lack of interest**
Not knowing the importance or variety of STEM careers.

If we don't get girls interested in STEM careers, how can we expect them to choose STEM subjects?

If we enrol girls in **STEM workshops**, and allow them to see women working and succeeding in their **Science, Technology, Engineering** and **Mathematics** careers, then girls will have real-world demonstrations to excite them and role models to inspire them.
Then more girls can…

dream **BIG**

What do Carpenters do?

Carpenters can build and repair things made out of wood, plastic, fibreglass, plasterboard and cement. They can work on a variety of different projects, from small bird-houses to **large** skyscrapers. Using simple tools like hammers, saws, drills, glue, measuring tapes and sandpaper, along with more high-tech tools like nail guns, air compressors, lathes and electric saws, Carpenters can build, repair and create many things.

Depending on which area a Carpenter works in, they will have different titles. **Finish** Carpenters create furniture and models. **Luthiers** work on stringed wooden musical instruments. **Ship** Carpenters build and repair ships. **Trim** Carpenters make and repair moulding and trim for doors and windows and finishing touches on ornamental pieces. **Restoration** Carpenters work on old buildings or structures, and **Scenic** Carpenters work on theatre and movie sets. All Carpenters should try to use sustainable materials to make their work energy-efficient and environmentally friendly. This is called '**green carpentry**'.

Carpenters work in lots of different places, but most of their work is in three main areas: **residential, commercial** or **industrial.** 'Residential' means apartments, condominiums, houses, flats, cabins, cottages, chalets, yurts, mansions, villas and castles. 'Commercial' means schools, hospitals, shopping centres and office blocks. **'Industrial'** means public civil settings like roads, mines, bridges, dams, tunnels or power plants.

Where can Carpenters work?

Carpenters can work in any country in the world, indoors and outdoors. They can work for themselves or for a contractor. They can also work on their own projects in their spare time, like toys, fancy birdhouses, coat stands or elaborately made furniture. They can sell their creations or give them away to family and friends. Carpenters can also donate their work and time to charities.

What's so great about Carpenters?

A Carpenter can help with the building of roads, skyscrapers and bridges. In just one house, they can build the frame, roof, stairs, floors, walls, doors, trim and kitchen cupboards, as well as the desks, chairs, tables, shelving, bookcases, wardrobes, beds, dressers and picture frames! Then outside, they can build play centres, swing sets, ponds, decking areas and even a tree house. A Carpenter can take an ordinary piece of wood and **transform** *it into many useful, beautiful and amazing things.*

Carpenters have skills!

Carpenter

car – pen – tur

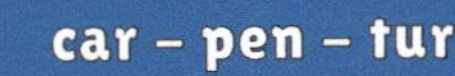

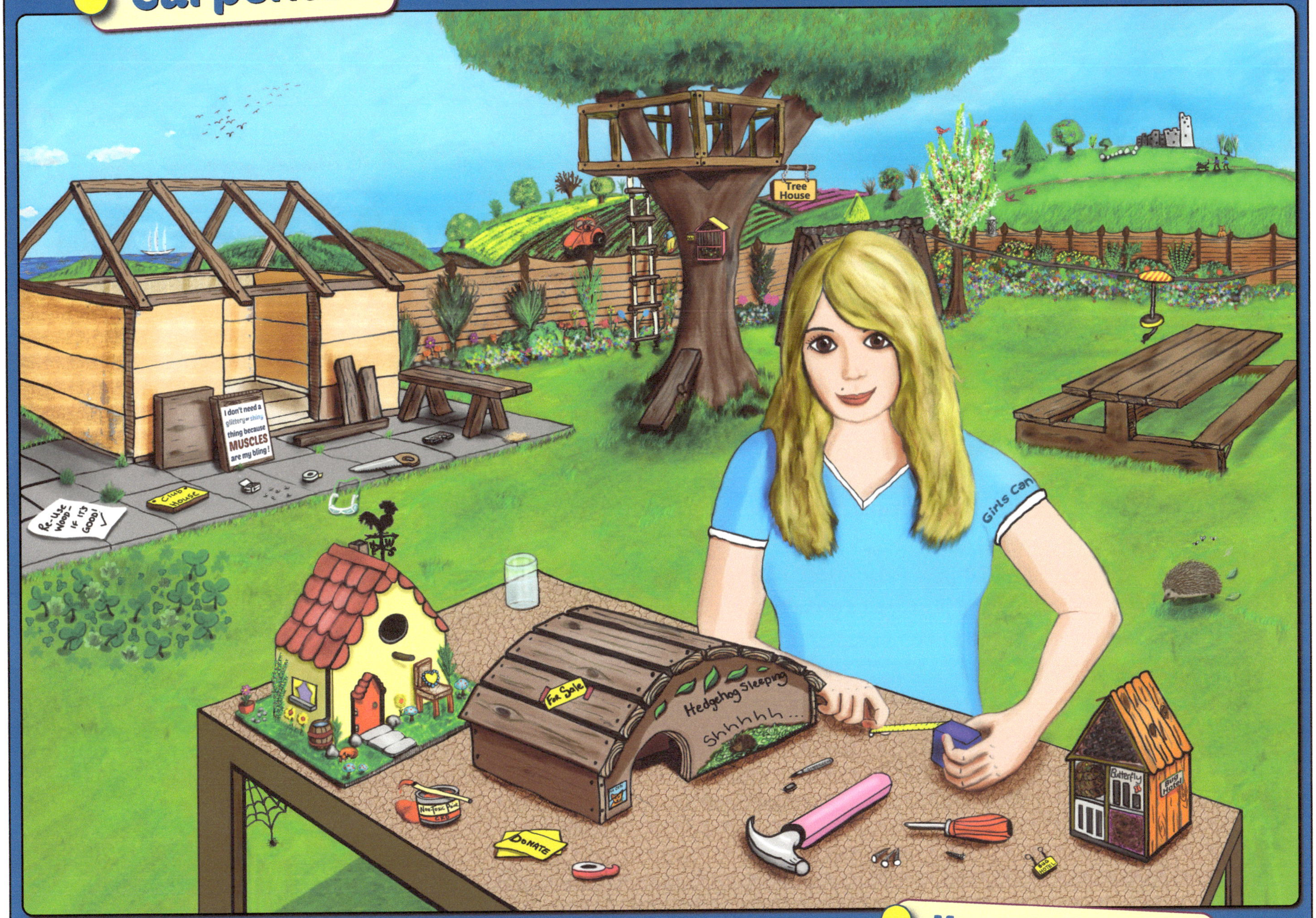

Measure – Saw – Build

What do Cartographers do?

Cartographers are mapmakers. They make maps that are easy to understand and interesting to look at. While **basic** maps show rivers, mountains, towns and countries, **special** maps can show where the most energy in the world is being used or how an animal population has changed in one area or where a disease is spreading. Cartographers make maps of outer space, tourist maps, maps showing the best location for a hospital or school, maps of which areas might flood in the future, maps for **amusement** parks, maps of where humans are richest or poorest, and even amazing **3D** maps. Cartographers can make maps of unusual things, like a map of the **smells** in a city, the **emotions** of a country or the **quietest** places on Earth.

Cartographers make maps that show people information that is easier to understand in **picture form**, rather than in words. You could read pages and pages of information about the amount of rainfall around the world, or just look at a map showing the amount of rainfall in each country, in different **colours**.

Cartographers can use computers and tablets. along with other technology, to research, design and create interesting maps. They **gather** information from different places, **check** if it is all correct and then decide how best to **display** it so that it helps as many people as possible.

Where can Cartographers work?

Cartographers can work in any country in the world. While most of the work is usually done indoors on computers, Cartographers can also do field work and collect or recheck data on a site. Cartographers can work for government agencies, private businesses and companies, and they can also teach at colleges and universities.

Weird Word of the Job

Isohyet

A line on a map that connects places that have the same amount of rainfall

What's so great about Cartographers?

Cartographers use science, art and technology every day. They use their maps to tell a story or display lots of information in just one picture. They can help us see where the noise and light levels of different cities are, so we can find places to build new houses that won't disturb the local wildlife. Cartographers could even help us decide where the best place to live on Mars would be! A map of countries that have the most sustainable forests and cleanest rivers could be helpful in deciding which countries could help those that are less sustainable. The maps of Cartographers could help the whole world.

Cartographers help us to learn beautifully and in pictures!

Cartographer
car – tog – rah – fur
Éire
MAPS
Notice Board
CHARITIES WE SUPPORT
LORNA BYRNE
CHILDRENS FOUNDATION
SIGHT SAVERS
ST. VINCENT DE PAUL
CkD Cartography
Our dreams Our Future...
LIDAR
ATLAS 3000
GEOGRAPHY IS INTERESTING
Knick Knack Basket Rack
Girls Can
CARTOGRAPHY AWARD
CkD Cartography
FILE: GIS ZeitGeis
CKD
ROADS
TREES
RIVERS
OFFICES
ALL
Geographical Information Systems (GIS)
Thank Steve
Satellite and Geodetic Information for IRELAND
2021 -'22
Revised and Updated By CKD Cartography
Liaise – Gather – Create

Ceramics Engineers are scientists. They use their knowledge and technology to create ceramics and find ways to make them stronger and more useful. **What are ceramics?** Ceramics are composed of non-metallic minerals and other substances taken from the ground, like **clay**, **mica**, quartz and **silica sand**. When they are processed with heat, water and other ingredients the material created is strong, tolerates heat and abrasion, and can be moulded into any needed shape. Ceramics Engineers experiment with different types of soil particles and mix different ingredients together to create better ceramics. Since ceramics make such good conductors and insulators, they are used in all sorts of electronic parts.

So many different items are made with ceramics, that our homes are filled with them! Toilets, glass, crockery and bricks contain ceramic elements, and so do washing machines, stoves, refrigerators, toasters, ovens, computers, tablets, headphones, mobile phones, solar panels and watches. You can also find ceramics in cement, heat reflective paints, hospital scanners, hearing aids, bone and teeth replacements, orthodontic braces, pacemakers, and artificial heart valves. Ceramics are also used in drill bits for drilling wells, water filters, lasers and fibre optics. Even your bicycle and tennis rackets contain ceramics mixed with plastic. Ceramics are so important and used in so many unseen ways, in many devices all around the world, that they are helping to make our technological lives better than ever before. I wonder what future devices we'll find them in?

Where can Ceramics Engineers work?

Ceramics Engineers can work all around the world, indoors and outdoors. They work in laboratories, glass companies, offices, mines and factories. They can work for governments and businesses or teach in universities. They can travel and work in sales and marketing, or conduct research. Ceramics Engineers can work in many areas including the electronics, mining, medical, automotive, aerospace, food, and chemical, industries.

Weird Word of the Job

composite

Made up of several parts or elements

What's so great about Ceramics Engineers?

Our modern society would be unable to advance without ceramics. They have helped medical, clean energy, electronics, engineering, telecommunications, and manufacturing industries to advance. Ceramics Engineers take material from the ground and process it into a strong, versatile and very useful substance. One day, Ceramics Engineers could help invent a giant **3D** *printer to make us personal robots, flying cars, healthy chocolate dispensers, or a soft and comfortable jumper that is as strong as a* **superheroes shield***!*

Ceramics Engineers are innovative!

Ceramics Engineer

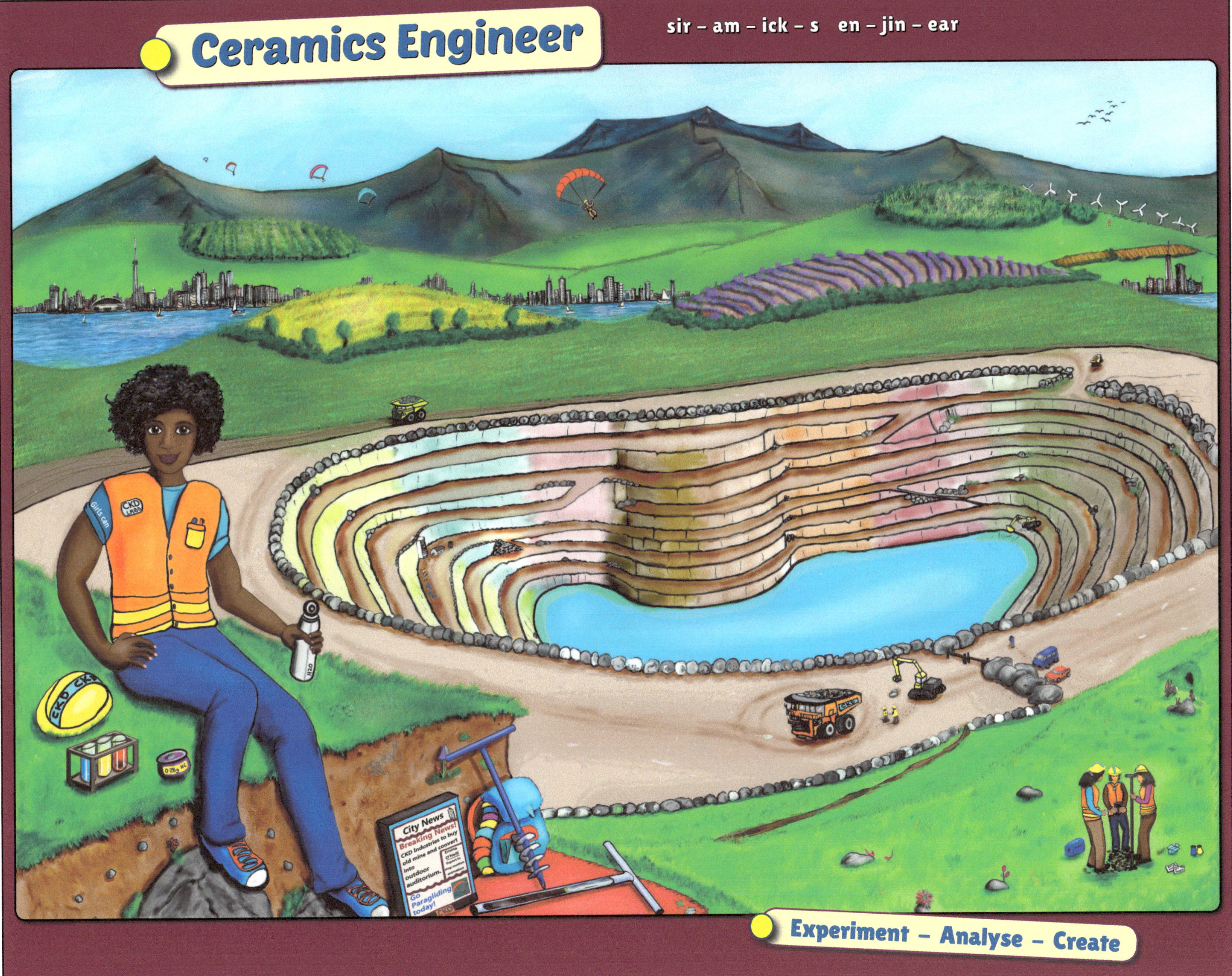

What do Data Scientists do?

A Data Scientist gathers and analyses large amounts of information to find patterns, problems or better ways of doing things. They use maths, statistics and computer programs to sort through sets of data. All companies, hospitals, governments and education systems generate massive amounts of information that could help them solve lots of problems. However, without Data Scientists to analyse, sort and research all of this information, it cannot be used to help anyone. Hospitals need to know how to improve health-care. Businesses need to find out how to deliver a better service. Plants and animals that are going extinct need Data Scientists to find ways to help them thrive again. The whole world needs to learn how to use resources like water and energy more efficiently. Before decisions are made on where to spend money, a Data Scientist can examine all of the information, so that money is not wasted on something that won't work.

Data Scientists can help governments and hospitals find the most productive ways to combat a virus outbreak. They can analyse data to help sports people improve their performance, prevent injuries and win more trophies! Data Scientists also **help charities** to better manage their resources and finances. They can find solutions to help combat homelessness, make emergency food deliveries more efficient or identify ways to increase financial donations.

Where can Data Scientists work?

A Data Scientist can work anywhere in the world, as most of the work is done indoors on a computer. Every country in the world has hospitals, governments, universities, colleges, companies and businesses that generate huge amounts of data. Since so much information is generated and used every day in our modern world, Data Scientists will always be needed to sort through it all, to help us find better ways to do almost everything.

Weird Word of the Job

quartile

a set of data divided

into	four
equal	parts

What's so great about Data Scientists?

Data Scientists can find problems before they start. They stop schools, colleges, governments, hospitals and businesses from making costly mistakes. They can help governments decide on the best course of action for spending tax money or to help combat virus outbreaks. Data Scientists could help to discover new ways to use renewable energy; find out how our climate is changing; or why some plants and animals are going extinct. Mental and physical health issues worldwide could be solved, if we have **enough information** *about how they start in the first place. Data Scientists can help the whole world and everyone in it.*

Data Scientists are incredible!

Data Scientist
day – tah   s – eye – en – t – ist
CKD DATA SCIENCE A GREAT PLACE TO WORK !
AWARD MENTAL HEALTH SERVICES 2021
CKD DATA SCIENCE
Processing data...
BOX A
? IDEAS
LED Bulbs
INK
Printer Paper
CODING
CKD LABWORKS
Model Number 02062019
Have a great day :)
CKD LABWORKS
Model Number : 0001062019
Have a nice day :)
Girls Can
Statistics on Irish Children
Mental Health Data
Helping Children
Research – Discover – Solve

What do Electricians do?

Electricians install, maintain and inspect wiring for electrical devices. They read blue-prints and can design wiring layouts for electrical systems. They use measuring tools, hand-held tools and climbing gear, and also hydraulic equipment to help them reach higher places like street lights or pylons. Sometimes they use heat-sensing equipment and infrared sensors, to make sure no part of the wiring is getting so hot as to cause a fire. Electricity can be created in renewable ways using our natural resources; the ocean, ground, wind and sun. (See Wind Engineer on page 34 for more details on how electricity is created).

Electricity is needed everywhere. Offices, schools, hospitals, restaurants, theatres, cinemas, shops, art galleries, factories, museums and theme parks require a great deal of electricity to provide services to us. In order for Ambulance staff to get their patients safely to the hospital, they need life-saving battery-operated equipment. Since batteries store electricity, they allow us to bring technology with us when we travel. Modern boats, cars and airplanes all have electronic parts too. Electricity is part of our daily lives, but we hardly notice it until it's suddenly gone...

I'll just browse the net on my tablet, while I'm waiting for the power to come back on. Oh wait, it's out of power! I'll just charge it. Ah, no! Power's gone. I'll play a game on my console. Ah, no power! I'll read a book. Ah, no lights! I'll use my flashlight. Ah, no batteries! I'll cook dinner then. Ah, no oven! Well, I'll just watch TV. Oh, wait ... no TV?! I'm going to bed!

Where can Electricians work?

Electricians can work around the world, indoors or outdoors, in residential, industrial, construction and commercial areas. They can work for private companies, governments, or for themselves. They can work in homes, businesses, wind farms, hospitals, factories, film and television, hydro-electric power plants, and space agencies. They can also work on vehicles, at concerts or aboard boats, airplanes and oil rigs.

Weird Word of the Job

negawat

unit of energy saved as a direct result of energy conservation

What's so great about Electricians?

Electricians have helped to modernise our world by powering our lights, technology and the internet. They give us the power to see in the dark, to stay warm or cool down, to learn, to get well in hospital, to create cleaner energy and communicate with each other all around the world and out into space, to share knowledge and experiences from culture to culture and from country to country. Electricians help make lots of other jobs possible too, and this has allowed us to have more scientific, engineering and technological break-throughs than ever before, so we can all live better lives.

Electricians help us to advance!

Electrician
ell – eck – tr– ish – an
Museum Café
Cable Castle Café
Rock of Castlemaise
Our dreams Our Future
CKD
CKD
CKD HYDRO
Girls can
Camp Site ONE
Welcome to Castlemaise Camp
Bird Rest
CKD ELECTRICS
Underground Electrics Phase 1
Blue Prints and Procedures
Pros-thetic wipes
Danger
OFF
ON
Wire – Power – Light

What do Geneticists do?

A Geneticist studies **genes**, but not the ones you wear (jeans). You have trillions of cells inside your body with a type of **acid** inside of them called DNA. The letters DNA are an abreviation for; 'DeoxyriboNucleic Acid' which you pronounce like this: dee-ox-ee-r-eye-bow-new-clay-ick acid. DNA is a set of instructions that tells a cell what to do. Genes are small sections of DNA strands. They determine lots of things in your body, like the **colour** of your hair and eyes, the **shape** of your ear-lobes and whether you get **freckles** or **dimples**. Some genes are fun, like whether you can roll your tongue or not. Some genes are more serious, like whether you can get a certain disease or not. All living things have DNA in their cells, not just people. Plants, animals and viruses have DNA too.

There are several branches of genetics for people to work in. An **Agricultural** Geneticist tries to find ways to make farmers' crops and plants grow healthier, bigger and more resistant to diseases. A **Biomedical** Geneticist tries to find out what makes people or animals sick. A **Forensic** Geneticist studies DNA found at crime scenes to figure out who is innocent and who is guilty. Lots of things from your body have **DNA** in them, like **blood**, **sweat**, **tears**, **skin**, **hair follicles**, **saliva**, **mucus** and **ear wax**. Everyone's DNA is different from everyone else's and this is part of what makes you,

completely unique!

Where can Geneticists work?

Geneticists can work in many countries around the world. They usually spend most of their time in laboratories and offices, where they consult with their patients and do research projects. Geneticists can work for hospitals, institutions, companies, businesses, universities, governments, or even in **zoos**, where they can help endangered animals have healthy babies.

What's so great about Geneticists?

The only way we can completely fix a body's problems is to find out exactly how every little part of that body works, and how it has failed. If DNA can show us where the problems are, then Geneticists can work out how to fix them. One day, all diseases could be cured, mental health problems could be prevented, our bodies could be much stronger, and our minds could absorb huge amounts of information, instantly!

Geneticists could make us all superhuman!

Geneticist
juh – net – uh – s – ist
CKD
Genetics Ltd.
TO HELP AND HEAL
CKD Industries
04 Laminar Flow Cabinet
SAFETY FIRST !
Always wear eye protectors
LARGE   MED   SMALL
Genetics
Genome
CATG
1 2 3
SAFETY FIRST !
Always wash your hands
EYE WASH
SOAP
ON OFF
Girls can
My Dream Career
CKD
CKD Monitors
Serial No. 11134852
Model No. 04000
For LAB use only
SLIDES
What's in our water ??
Detect – Study – Report

What do Glassblowers do?

Glassblowers are glass artists. They blow into a blob of molten hot glass through a tube, then roll, shape, pull, pinch and twist it into beautiful, unique and valuable items. Glassblowers also make glass tubes and apparatus for scientists. Glassblowers have to work near a **furnace** that is hot enough (over 1400 degrees Celsius) to melt sand, soda and lime together to make glass. You cook a cake in an oven at 180 degrees Celsius, so a normal oven would never do! A special oven called an **annealer** is necessary to **s l o w l y** cool down the blown glass because if it's cooled *too fast* it could crystallise and won't be transparent anymore, or it could crack.

Glassblowers use a marver – a table with a polished steel top that won't melt or burn when the molten glass touches it. Glassblowers use **jacks, paddles, shears** and **blow pipes** to shape the glass. **Colours** have to be added in before the glass cools down and hardens, so coloured glass dust, or coloured pieces of glass called '**canes**', are added while the glass is still molten hot, so they blend together well. Glassblowers create stunning **trophies, bowls, jewellery, presentation awards, ornaments, figurines, vases,** and **lamps,** with amazing patterns and designs. As a result of the blowing, the handling and the variety of colouring treatments, each one of their creations is,

a unique work of art

Where can Glassblowers work?

Glassblowers can work in many countries around the world. They usually work for themselves in glass-making studios or for glass factories and museums. They can also teach glass-blowing to others. Scientific Glassblowers can work in universities, colleges, private companies, businesses or hospitals, to make and repair those uniquely shaped glass tubes and flasks that all Scientists use for experiments in their laboratories.

What's so great about Glassblowers?

Glassblowers shape glass into beautiful, useful and unique items that are **highly prized** as collector pieces. They create trophies for lots of major sports championships, and awards for some really amazing people. Scientists and Chemists would be unable to conduct some experiments, without a Glassblower to make glass equipment. Glassblowers have helped to make the first **thermometers, light bulbs** and **televisions.** Glassblowing is an ancient art that has been in use for over 2000 years.

Glassblowers are cool
even though they work with a hot furnace!

Glassblower
g – lass – blow – er
Heat Blocker 2000
CKD Industries
CKD GLASSWORKS
All life is in our hands
RODS
CANES N' RODS
RODS N' CANES
Girls can
Girls can
Knick Knack Basket Rack
Knick Knack
Madi Pack
Blow – Turn – Create

What do Hydrologists do?

Hydrology is the study of water and its impact on our planet. Hydrologists are scientists. They examine and solve **water** problems. They research all of the interesting ways in which water travels from one place to another, picking up nutrients or pollutants along the way, eroding mountains, flooding fields and towns, or leaving some areas too dry. Hydrologists investigate how water can help or hinder any animal, plant or human life it meets as it journeys along rivers, to sea, to sky and to underground lakes along the way. Whether it's a town needing a **flood** management plan, a **polluted** water supply in a farmer's field, a or a new community of people needing a **fresh** water source; a Hydrologist can figure out all of the solutions that are needed.

They use a variety of tools and science equipment in their work. Hydrologists test water samples, of course, but they also use computer software and even drones to help solve water problems. Drones can fly over areas that are too difficult for people to access or just too large for one person alone to monitor. A Hydrologist can work in a variety of settings. They can wade through a river to take soil and water samples, research and design a solution on computer or meet with other scientists to do research. Hydrologists analyse data on environmental impacts like drought and pollution. They also write reports and proposals and then have meetings with clients, so they can work out solutions to any problems they find and how much they will cost to fix.

Where can Hydrologists work?

Hydrologists can work indoors and outdoors in any country in the world. Since people, plants and animals everywhere need and use water, Hydrologists can work for many different sectors like engineering companies, private land owners, governments, private research companies, environmental agencies and consultancies, and any other businesses that supply or manage water.

What's so great about Hydrologists?

Water is precious and all life needs it, but so do clothes, bicycles, ketchup and car factories. Almost everything we eat, wear and use needs water to produce it. We also use water for swimming, boating and kayaking. All of these uses for water need to have plans to manage them or the water sources can become polluted, cause flooding or dry up completely. Hydrologists help us find efficient ways to use our water sources. They also help the animals and plants that use the water too, so we can all have a positive and viable future.

Hydrologists help sustain all life

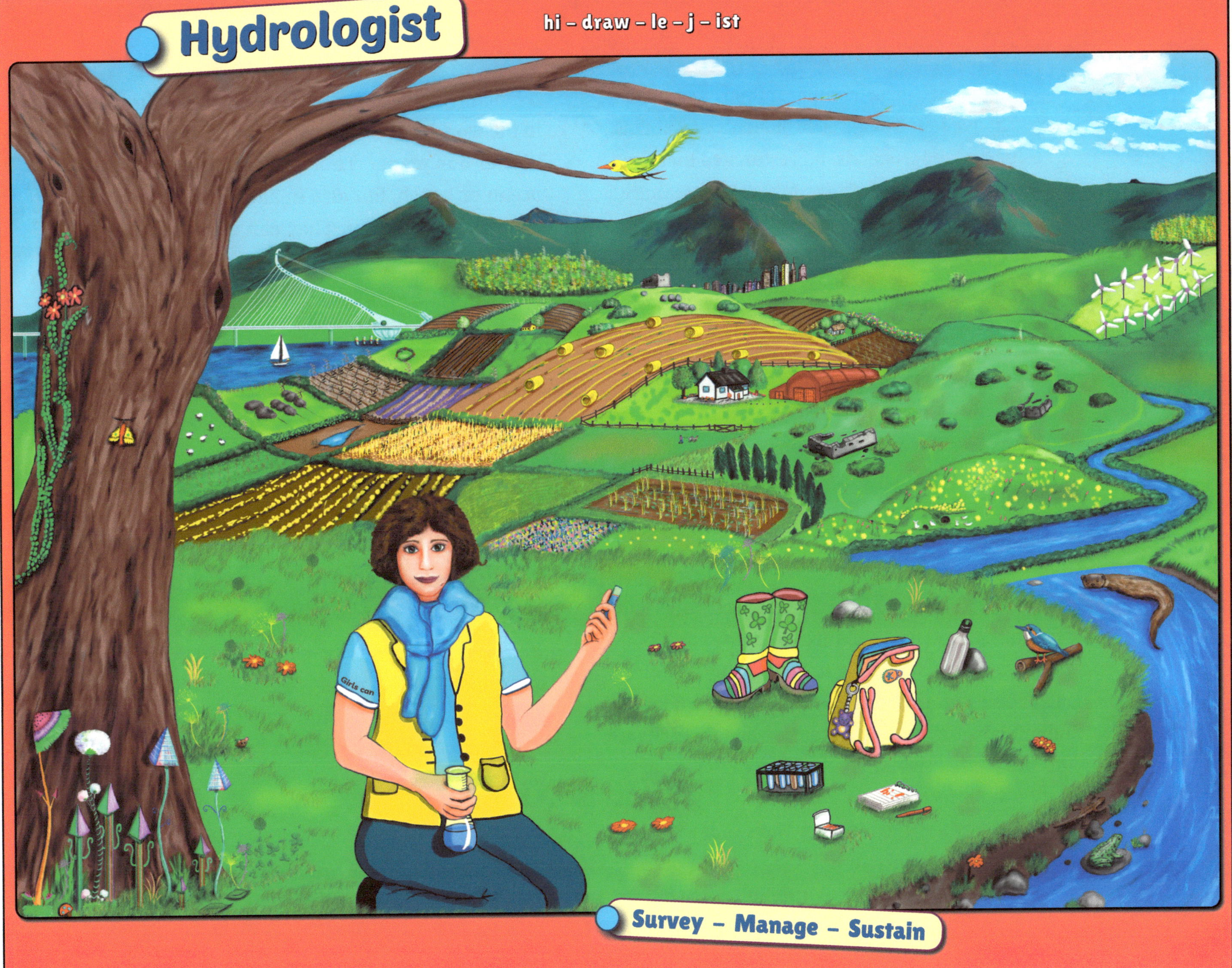
Hydrologist
hi – draw – le – j – ist
Girls can
Survey – Manage – Sustain

What do Marine Biologists do?

Marine Biologists monitor animals and plants that live in saltwater environments like oceans, estuaries and wetlands. It is estimated that over **one million different species** live in the world's oceans, so a Marine Biologist has a great choice of which area to study or specialise in. They can study the migratory habits of **HUGE** whales or sharks or monitor tiny microscopic organisms to learn more about how they affect our atmosphere. (**Phytoplankton** are microscopic creatures that live in the sea and produce about 50% of the air we breathe.)

Marine Biologists can travel the oceans to monitor giant squid and narwhals or they can stay in one area to study how certain creatures, like sea lions for example, feed and care for their babies. Marine Biologists can also monitor the habitats that sea creatures live in and research how **environmental factors** affect different creatures and their habitats, like plastic polluting the oceans and how fish (and humans) are eating it. Marine Biologists can also analyse seismic fault lines on the ocean floor or find out how tiny creatures survive and thrive near **underwater volcanoes**. They can even investigate the effects of man-made disasters, like oil spills, and try to discover ways that can help minimise or prevent damage to the oceans and all the sea life contained in them.

Where can Marine Biologists work?

A Marine Biologist can work almost anywhere in the world, because oceans cover more than 70% of our planet. They can work near an ocean or beach, but also in a laboratory, a zoo or an aquarium. They can work for governments, universities, companies and consulting firms, and also national parks and non-profit organisations. Sometimes, Marine Biologists are needed to work on rescue missions.

Weird Word of the Job

phototactic
moving in response to light

What's so great about Marine Biologists?

They get a chance to work aboard submarines or boats, with remote-controlled sea vehicles that have grabbing arms to pick up samples (**or treasure!**) from the ocean floor. When on the water, Marine Biologists wear life-jackets for safety. Scuba diving may also be part of their job. Their work tools include underwater cameras, nets and traps for plant and animal collection, instruments for recording and measuring, computers, tablets and specialised software programs. With the help of Marine Biologists, we might discover amazing new sea creatures, develop medicines from a newly discovered ocean plant, or even find cures for diseases.

Marine Biologists help protect ocean life.

Marine Biologist

mar – een   bye – oll – ah – j – ist

Analyse – Ocean – Life

What do Photographers do?

Professional Photographers take pictures, either for clients or to license them for a fee. The photos can be of events and magical moments, beautiful views of landscapes and cityscapes, or of any people, animals and objects the public might be interested in. Photographers learn how lighting, camera equipment and computer software can be used to create amazing pictures. Most people just look at things, but a good Photographer sees the beauty or magic of what they are looking at and then tries to capture it on camera.

There are dozens of different areas for Photographers to specialise in. A **Photojournalist** takes photos that are used to tell a story in pictures, usually about current news topics from around the world, sometimes in dangerous places. **Equine** Photographers take photos of horses and their owners. **Astrophotographers** capture images of objects in outer space. **Action** photographers take photos of fast moving sports. **Macro** photographers take pictures of objects up close, and **Photomicrographers** take photos of tiny objects under a microscope. **Fashion** photographers take photos of models wearing designer clothes. Newspapers, museums, art galleries and magazines all need photos for websites or printed materials. Architects and realtors need photos of buildings or land they are hoping to sell. **Aerial** Photographers take pictures from a plane, a helicopter or even a hot air balloon. They can also float through the sky in a parachute, taking photos of skydivers.

Now, I bet you can guess what **Wildlife** Photographers, **Wedding** Photographers, **Science** Photographers and **Medical** Photographers take pictures of!

Where can Photographers work?

Photographers can work in every country in the world, indoors or outdoors. They can work for businesses, individuals, governments, research facilities or for themselves. They are also employed by travel companies, universities, colleges, museums and hospitals. They can work in the fashion world and the movie and television industry. Photographers can also work in holiday resorts and aboard cruise ships.

What's so great about Photographers?

*Photographers can take pictures of things that are too fast, too small or too far away for us to see with just our eyes. Lightning bolts, a microscopic strand of DNA or a new planet millions of miles away can all be seen, thanks to Photographers. They show you an emotion or tell you a story in just one picture. They are **artists**. By taking photos, they learn to understand more about themselves and the things they love and value – and they share that **knowledge** with us through their pictures. They also gain knowledge of the real beauty in the world by noticing incredible details in the pictures they take. Photographers capture moments that speak to us without words, without language, without barriers. They speak to our humanity.*

Photographers help us to really see

Photographer
foe – tog –rah – fur
Girls can
Look – See – Capture

What do Psychologists do?

Psychology is a branch of science that deals with the study of thought, emotion and behaviour. A Psychologist is like a doctor of the mind. They want to help people discover what has caused their problems and how to solve them. They study brain functions and mental processes, and also the interactions and behaviours of individuals, groups and environments. There are different fields of psychology, including forensic, cognitive, clinical, behavioural, counselling and developmental. Depending on which field they work in, Psychologists perform a wide range of duties. They design and conduct studies, analyse data and research new techniques to help treat their clients and patients. Some Psychologists conduct laboratory experiments, administer questionnaires and surveys, and conduct interviews. They can also design programmes on public health information and help a company's products and technologies become more user-friendly.

Psychology is a diverse field with many overlapping areas of application and research. There are sub-fields and areas to specialise in. **Sports** Psychology helps athletes and dancers adjust to being injured or to deal with performance anxiety. **Cyberpsychology** explores the impact technology and social media have on people's values and behaviour. **Child** Psychologists help children with emotional or developmental problems. **Engineering** Psychologists study how technology, machines and work environments can be improved, for example, by discovering ways to adapt equipment for people with disabilities. **Environmental** Psychologists study the relationship between people and their surroundings, either built or natural. **Consumer** Psychologists examine behaviours to discover why our thoughts and feelings make us choose the things we buy.

Where can Psychologists work?

Psychologists can work all around the world, in clinics, hospitals, governments, schools, colleges, universities, commercial and industrial companies, and consulting firms. They also work in facilities that provide more immediate support for people who need it, such as rehabilitation, mental health clinics, and crisis centres for victims of abuse. They can also travel around the world to attend conferences, learn about the latest research and find new or better ways to treat their patients and help their clients.

Weird Word of the Job

distressor
a negative event that is stressful

What's so great about Psychologists?

*When someone feels sad, confused, depressed or anxious, a Psychologist can help. They listen to problems, and help find causes and solutions. Psychologists use research, clinical findings and new treatment therapies in order to help people. They **improve** school and working environments, **guide** governmental health policies and legislation, and **discover** how we as a society can live our lives in a happier and more productive way. Whether Psychologists are therapists, researchers, consultants or advisors, they are always working to help improve lives.*

Psychologists help us to understand

Psychologist
s – eye – call – ah – j – ist
Things I cannot control
Things I CAN control
Listen – Understand – Help

What do Robotics Engineers do?

Robotics Engineers research, design, create and maintain robots and robotic parts, and the software that controls them. Robotic creations can be used for fun or to help people do things better, faster and more safely than ever before. Robotics are used in theme parks; in space; below the ocean; inside factories, hospitals, and vehicles; on search and rescue missions; and even in your clothes! One example of this is electronic ID chips that can be sewn inside clothing, to tell a **smart washing machine** how best to wash that garment. Robotics Engineers can also work with other types of engineers to create devices to help people that have physical limitations or impairments.

Robotics Engineers can help design and build tools, vehicles and equipment to help us explore deep oceans on Earth and other planets. They create robots that can sort and recycle waste products that are not safe for people to touch. Robots that are used in manufacturing plants and factories, have precision tools that are so efficient there is **less wastage**. Driverless cars could one day help people to be safer on the roads and more productive too. You'll be able to check your email while your car drives you to work!

Remote-controlled robots, like drones, can be used to cover large distances **more quickly and safely** than humans. They can **fly** items to people in remote places, **inspect** areas on huge structures like bridges and buildings, and **search** for lost or injured people over a large area. Drones can also help us to **track** river flows, flooding, forest fires or endangered species that are all difficult to observe from the ground.

Where can Robotics Engineers work?

Robotics Engineers work all over the world, usually indoors in a laboratory, factory or office setting. Robotics Engineers can work for governments, colleges, universities or companies, or they can make their own devices at home to experiment on, sell or donate to charity. They can travel abroad to attend conferences and discover new and better ways of creating robotic devices.

Weird Word of the Job

gimbal

A pivoted support that allows the rotation of an object in multiple directions

What's so great about Robotics Engineers?

*Robotics Engineers make robotic parts that are very helpful. They can make moving artificial arms for hospital patients or astronauts on **Mars**, or a robot that can safely work in places where humans cannot. Drones can fly medicine to an injured climber hundreds of miles from help. **Robotics** can make things easier, safer and more efficient for us.*

*One day you could have a **jacket** with built in solar panels for charging your devices, that can change colour at the touch of a button, play your favourite music, let you chat with your friends, keep you dry when it rains, heat you up when you're cold, and cook a meal when you're hungry!*

Robotics Engineers create amazing futures!

Robotics Engineer

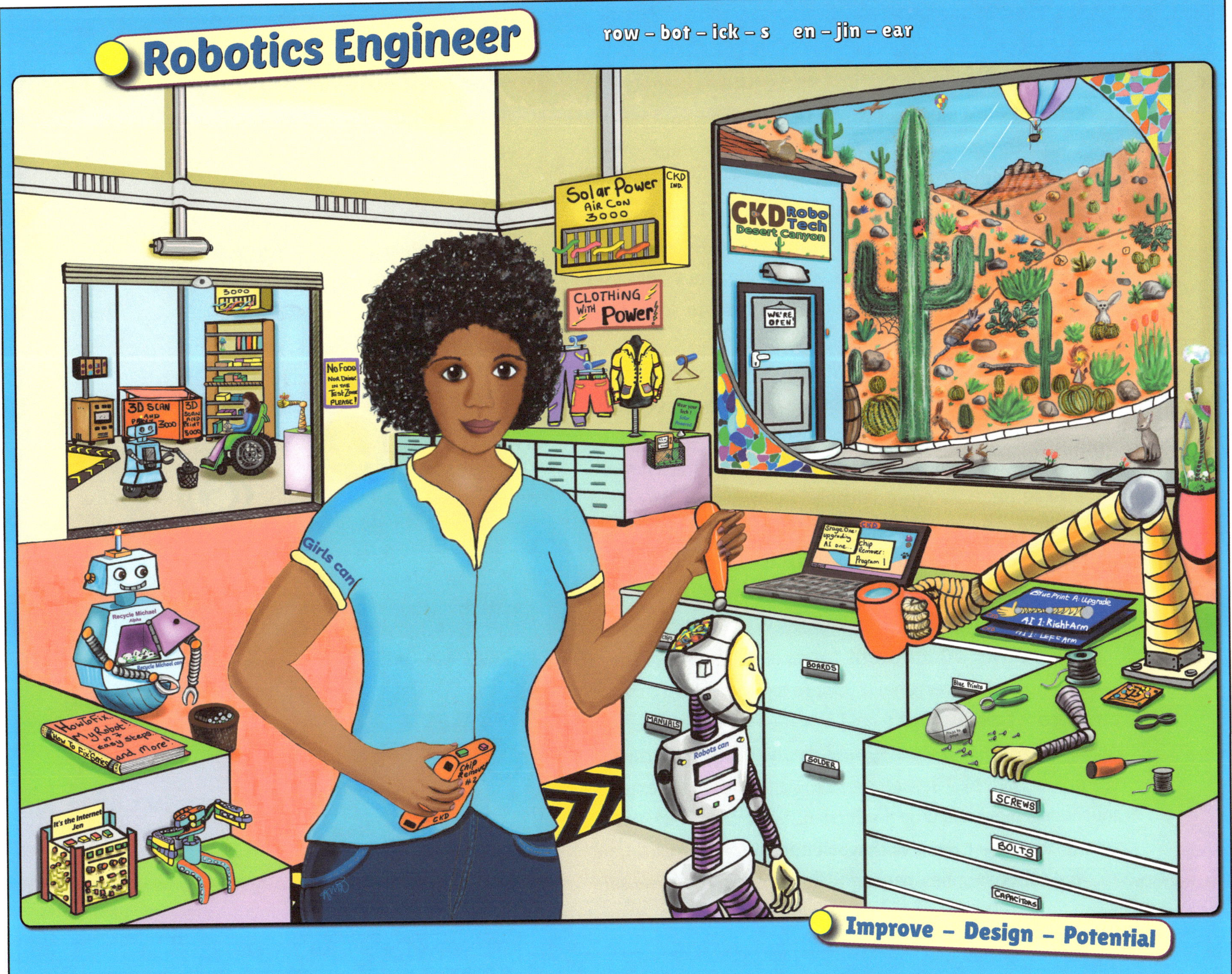

What do Scientists do?

Scientists are curious people; they like to know exactly how things work. They research information, set up experiments, conduct investigations and prepare reports. They use a standard technique for uncovering a truth, called 'the scientific method'. This means they make a guess (hypothesis) about an idea they have and then they research this idea and conduct tests to see if they are right or wrong.

Scientists are investigating alternative ways to manufacture things to see if we can create less waste, and how we might use different methods to reuse our waste and this may help to keep plastics out of the ocean. They are also helping to stop endangered animals from becoming extinct and figuring out ways to stop diseases from spreading. Scientists are also studying what is causing the climate to change and how we can use water, power and sunlight more efficiently.

There are over **80 different types** of Scientists, so there is something for everyone! If you are trying to find a cure for an infectious disease, you would be called an Epidemiologist. An Astronomer or Astrophysicist studies space. Bacteria and cells are studied by Microbiologists. Agronomists are experts in soil management and crop production. A Horticulturist studies plant life and a Conservation Scientist studies forests, land and water supplies, helping to keep our environment safe for us and future generations.

Where can Scientists work?

Scientists can work indoors and outdoors in every country in the world, in laboratories, offices, fields and caves, or on oceans and mountain tops. Scientists can work aboard hot air balloons, planes and space ships. They can work for hospitals, governments, food companies, colleges, universities, businesses and charities.

Weird Word of the Job

tribology

the study of friction and wear between surfaces

What's so great about Scientists?

Scientists have helped to create, discover and invent so many things, like medicines, technologies and communication devices that touch every corner of our lives. These scientific discoveries have helped us to stay healthier, live longer and discover amazing things about ourselves and the planet we live on. Scientists have helped us to talk to people all around the world and send signals and vehicles to other planets. They help to care for our planet by studying the climate and what's causing it to change, by discovering new solutions to pollution problems, and by figuring out new and better ways to reduce and recycle waste products. Science helps us understand so many things. Our modern world would not exist without them. In fact, our future world may not exist without them!

Scientists are indispensable!

Scientist

Solar Power
AIR CON
3000
CKD IND.
CKD
LABORATORIES
The Periodic Table of the Elements
Manifold
CKD
FE
Girls
can
CKD 1
20 20 06
To: CKD LABS
Tower One
Big City
Replacing Gas
Burners with
electric:
Stage One:
KNICK KNACK BASKET RACK
KNICK KNACK BASKET RACK
KNICK KNACK MEDI PACK
First
AID
KIT
The Cure
LIFT
OPEN
Stage 17...
Distillation
Techniques

What do Surgeons do?

Surgeons are doctors that specialise in operating on sick or injured people to help make them better. If medicines alone can't cure someone, a Surgeon will perform surgery to heal them. If, for example, a child's tonsils get infected, then a Surgeon can take out the tonsils so the child will never get sick in that way again. If a baby was born with a mouth that couldn't close properly, a surgeon could repair it. Surgeons use small specialised tools to fix our bodies, like scissors, scalpels, staplers and clamps, and larger tools like saws and drills. Right now, researchers are finding ways to make tiny robots (called 'nanobots') that go inside our bodies and fix problems from the inside. Surgeons will be able to control these nanobots and this makes repairing the human body much easier and quicker.

Surgeons can specialise in certain fields, and some parts of them overlap. **Cardiothoracic** Surgeons treat the heart and other chest organs such as the lungs, oesophagus and trachea. **Cosmetic** Surgeons can be called on to perform a surgery in a way that enhances or improves appearance or avoids scarring (for example, repairing an injured lip). **Neurosurgeons** deal with a patient's brain and nervous system. **Reconstructive** Surgeons work at restoring a person's appearance or the function of their organs, after they've had an accident or disfiguring illness. **Orthopaedic** Surgeons treat patients' bones, muscles and ligament problems. All surgeons care for their patients after surgery too. They check to make sure their patients are healing well, eating the right foods, and taking their medicine.

Where can Surgeons work?

Surgeons can work anywhere in the world, wherever there is a sterile environment, like hospitals. They can work for governments, institutions and in private practice, or do volunteer or paid work for charity groups that help victims of war or natural disasters. For example, if there was an earthquake, Surgeons could help set up mobile surgeries to treat people. They can also teach in universities or work in research settings, to find better ways to help patients.

What's so great about Surgeons?

*Surgeons can remove any diseased parts of the body that are causing problems and they can **repair** damage caused by accidents and injuries. Surgeons can **fix** some physical problems that people are born with, like a **cleft palate**, a **hernia** or an **extra finger**. They can transplant organs from one person to another to save their lives and they can even **sepa-rate** conjoined twins. Surgeons work to ease suffering and help sick, injured and impaired people live longer and better lives.*

Surgeons make a huge difference!

Surgeon
s – ur – jin
Ocean View Children's Hospital
Recovery Room 2
Joey
Paediatric Patrick
No keener cleaner
a sector by sector, disinfector
The energetic, non-magnetic
antiseptic cybernetic
with a sit-tight burning bright
sanitising UV light!
CKD Murals
Auto Soap
THEATRE VIEW
CKD MURALS
01-765-452
H2O
Ocean Mural   Operating Room   2   CKD Mechanics   Wide Glide Door Slide
OPERATING ROOM 2
SENSOR
TEAM 2 Result
Girls can
Scrub – Operate – Repair

What do Video Game Designers do?

Video Game Designers create games for our consoles. They come up with an idea and story for a game and work on the main ideas, for example, what the layout and characters might look like. Video Game Designers sketch drawings, write scripts and create story boards in order to show the other team members how their game might look and play. They also work out the cost of making the game and how long it will take to get the game ready to sell. Then the game needs to be advertised, so short sequences have to be created and edited, in order to see what the gameplay will be like. If a game looks exciting and fun, you'll probably want to play it. There are many careers involved in the **gaming industry**. Video Game Designers can work with as many as one hundred other people on a game. **Artists** draw and design characters on paper or computers, or even sculpt them in clay. **Programmers** need to transform these ideas and drawings into computer code. **Writers** have to weave an interesting story and all of the characters' dialogues. **Sound Designers** are needed to create musical backgrounds, sound effects and characters' voices. Finally, **Game Testers** play the game over and over to see if they can find any problems or glitches, and to make sure it's fun to play. Game Designers are at the **start** of the whole process though. They bring their **ideas to life** in the gaming world and create **memorable** games that are popular and **entertaining** for people of all ages and all walks of life.

Where can Video Game Designers work?

Video Game Designers can work around the world, usually indoors. Sometimes, they work in an office building with lots of rooms for all of the other team members that are part of the game design process. They can also work from home and use email, phones and video conferencing, to contact work colleagues and keep up to date with ongoing projects.

Weird Word of the Job

bevelling
the process of creating rounded edges on a mesh

What's so great about Video Game Designers?

Video Game Designers use their imagination and abilities to create exciting worlds, with characters to love, mysteries to solve and lessons to learn. They can offer us puzzles and prizes or pitfalls and perils along the way. Video Game Designers create games that help people learn new skills, like **improving memory** *and* **hand–eye coordination**. *Games help bring friends together to socialise, laugh and play, but they also teach us how to* **use resources**, **delegate tasks** *and* **work as part of a team**. *Video Game Designers create worlds for us to escape to, where we can be queens or warriors, animal rescuers or alien enemies – all in the same day!*

Video Game Designers are imaginative!

Video Game Designer

What do Wind Energy Engineers do?

Wind Energy Engineers design, build and maintain wind turbines. In order to make electricity, windmills and wind turbines use **kinetic** energy from the wind. 'Kinetic' means movement. Wind turbines are turned by the wind's **kinetic energy**. Inside the turbine, a gear box and a generator convert that kinetic energy into an electric current. It's a bit like the effect of a dynamo on a bicycle wheel. You cycle fast, the wheel spins, and you create enough power to turn on the dynamo's light. Wind turbines generate enough power to turn on many more lights! Wind is free and creates sustainable, renewable energy. Turbines can be placed on **mountains**, **oceans**, **open land** and **deserts**, and this means people in remote places can have access to electricity. Using electricity made from renewable sources creates less CO_2 gas (harmful carbon dioxide). This helps in the fight against global warming and climate change. There are a number of different ways to create renewable energy from our environment. Heat from under the ground can create steam that gives us **geothermal** electricity; sunlight makes **solar** electricity; moving water creates **hydroelectricity**; and ocean waves create **tidal** electricity.

A **wind farm** is a group of wind turbines together. If set up on a farmer's land, these turbines don't take up much space, so the farmer can still farm the land around them. Since the farmers earn money from having the turbines on their land, they can still earn money when there is a **drought** or **flooding** and their crops cannot grow. Wind Energy Engineers research all of the work that's involved in setting up a wind farm, like making sure the area will get enough wind blowing through, how tall the turbines need to be, and how the electricity will get to the power grid so people can use it.

Where can Wind Energy Engineers work?

Wind Energy Engineers can work indoors in offices, laboratories and factories, or outdoors on turbines that are on land or out on the ocean. They work all around the world for governments, charities and businesses. Wind Energy Engineers can also travel to meet with clients or to survey potential sites for wind farm and turbine placement.

What's so great about Wind Energy Engineers?

*Wind Energy Engineers can work with a team of other **STEM** people to design better ways of using wind energy. They can help to make our planet **cleaner** for ourselves and future generations. Wind Energy Engineers can help design **better** turbines that are **less visible**, **quieter** and **safer** for local wildlife. They can help make turbines less expensive to set up, so that more countries can use them.*

*Our planet, and all life on it, **benefits** greatly from using clean, and renewable energy. Wind Energy Engineers can help all countries to be more **eco-friendly**.*

Wind Energy Engineers are eco-warriors!

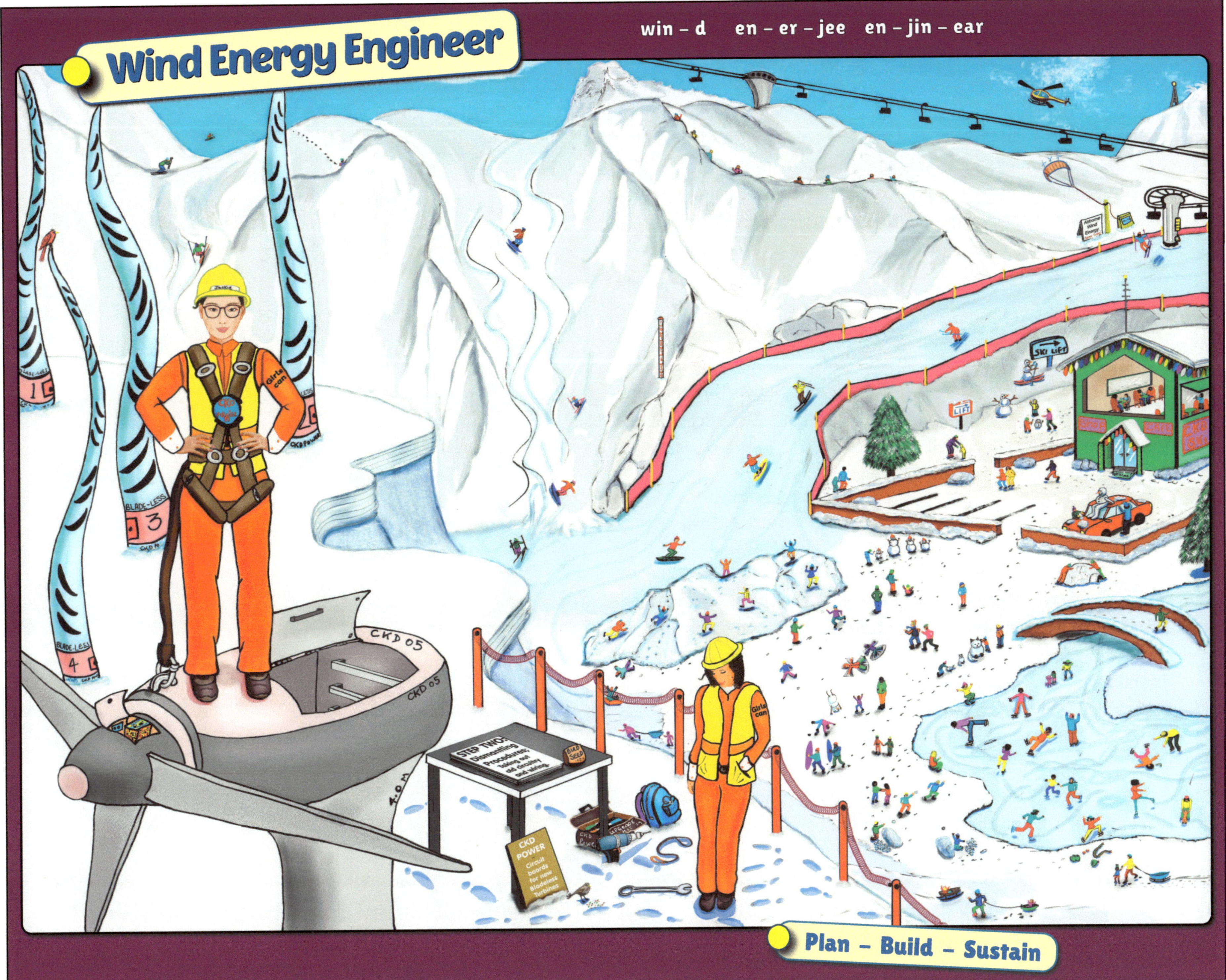
Wind Energy Engineer
win – d   en – er – jee   en – jin – ear
Plan – Build – Sustain
Girls can
SKI LIFT
LIFT
STEP TWO
CKD 05
CKD POWER
35

Having a friend

It's such an important thing in life to have someone believe in you. Friends do that. They make us feel special. Sometimes, a friend is your own age. Sometimes, a friend is someone you are related to, like a parent, sibling or cousin. Some friends are online, living in other countries. While friends come in different shapes and sizes, they all have one thing in common – they love you, they support you, they make you feel like you are important and that you matter. They may or may not say they love you, but they absolutely feel it. Every single person on this planet is important, but sometimes, people need a friend to tell them that, especially when they are sad. While it's great to have a friend, it's also great to be a friend. Supporting someone and helping them when they need it … well that's just priceless! In a world with so many people, it's easy to get lost in the crowd, but a friend can help you navigate your way.

A friend can make all the difference.

Girls that grow up and get STEM jobs don't have a lot of girl friends in STEM, because more men work there. But if girls stick together, if they support each other, if they help each other to succeed, then more girls will get STEM jobs. More girls will have more STEM girl friends and they won't feel so alone. Then the world will start to balance out. You can actually help to make this happen. You can make a difference in this world. All you have to do is start helping other girls, encourage them, cheer for them, support them and ask them to support you. Girls can support each other at home, in school, in work and in life; and the whole world will benefit from this.

If girls support girls and women support women, then we will all rise together.

Think of your favourite career picture and draw what it might look like with you in it.

What are you doing? How is your career helping? Are you using any tools? What's the weather like where you work? Are you standing on snow, cement, grass, wood or something else? Do you have any friends working with you?

Are you happy?

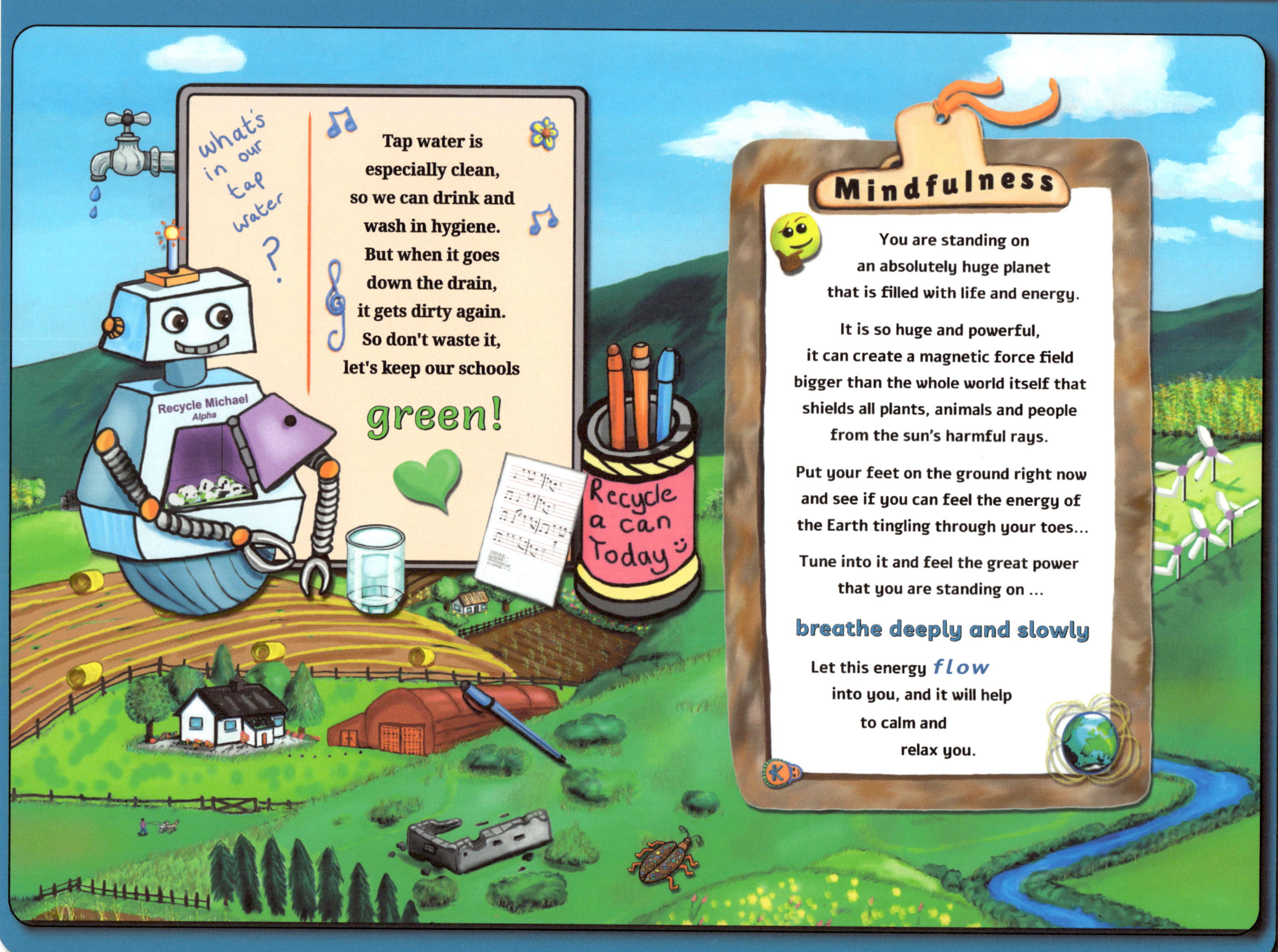

what's in our tap water ?

Tap water is
especially clean,
so we can drink and
wash in hygiene.
But when it goes
down the drain,
it gets dirty again.
So don't waste it,
let's keep our schools
green!

Recycle Michael
Alpha

Recycle a can Today

Mindfulness

You are standing on
an absolutely huge planet
that is filled with life and energy.

It is so huge and powerful,
it can create a magnetic force field
bigger than the whole world itself that
shields all plants, animals and people
from the sun's harmful rays.

Put your feet on the ground right now
and see if you can feel the energy of
the Earth tingling through your toes...

Tune into it and feel the great power
that you are standing on ...

breathe deeply and slowly

Let this energy flow
into you, and it will help
to calm and
relax you.

Girls can have great careers, so why not dream big?

My favourite careers so far are ...

I like them because ...

If I was in charge I would make the world better by ...

Some careers that might help me with that are ...

Hi there! My name is Anne Daly, and I am the author and illustrator of this book.

I was born in 1969 and raised on the north side of Dublin. I have worked in Ireland and North America, in management and the STEM sector, building, repairing, and troubleshooting computers. After a 16-year career and 10 years of marriage, I was 34 years old and ready to be a mother. I had two healthy babies (who are now teenagers) and I credit them for inspiring in me a passion to help children understand life. This has become the driving force behind my books.

I love nothing more than to settle down and explain things to a young child. They are like sponges absorbing information. If they start to lose interest after an hour or so, I still don't stop until I'm sure they fully understand. That kind of dedication and tenacity has helped my children become the expert eye-rollers they are today. I now live in the middle of Ireland in a little bungalow with my husband of 25 years, our two talented eye-rollers, three spoiled cats, and a big loud dog. I love nature, puzzle books and, of course, ~~explaining~~ chocolate.

Thanks for reading **Careers for Girls**. If you would like some free, printable items with this book's characters and themes, then please visit the 'Printables' page at www.AnneDaly.com. And if you enjoyed this book, can you please give it a positive review wherever you purchased it? Thank you!

Anne is now working on 'Careers for Girls Colouring Book' and 'Careers for Little Girls.' And also a book about the 37 stray cats she has adopted, fed, fostered and re-homed, over the past 20 years. Find out more at, **www.AnneDaly.com**.

How good can new technologies designed for women actually be, if women are not even consulted about the designs? Innovations and discoveries in STEM help populations advance and thrive, so when you consider

50% of the world's population is female

then it is very important that they have a greater say in what is ultimately going to affect, at least

Thank you!

Thank you to my husband and our children for their valuable help, support and never-ending patience while I worked on this book.

Thank you to my sisters for their help – Caroline, Geraldine, Grainne and Trasy. You are all brilliant and talented women I admire greatly!

Thank you to Sharon Lombard for kindly granting permission to quote from the eye-opening iWish 2017 Girls in STEM survey (www.iWish.ie). Thank you, ladies of iWish - you rock! And you rock girls' worlds.

Thank you to Professor Mark Ferguson, director general of Science Foundation Ireland, for allowing me to use a quote from his interview with an Irish newspaper. (www.irishexaminer.com/lifestyle/arid-20416606.html)

Thank you to Sandra Mulhall, the kind and wonderful teacher in Laois, who asked the question that started this book: 'What do you want to be when you grow up?'

Many thanks to my talented editor, Stephanie Campion. Thanks to psychologist Hollie Duff, psychotherapist Alison Power and psychiatrist Penny Rogers for their very much appreciated help.

And finally, thanks to you, the reader, for understanding the importance of helping young girls to,

dream BIG

"In all the ways of life, the man and woman should walk hand in hand; the one without the other is but half, each has a work to do."

Aquarian Gospel